**HAL LEONARD
STUDENT
PIANO
LIBRARY**

Broadway and Movie Hits

Arranged by
Fred Kern, Carol Klose, and Mona Rejino

Broadway and Movie Hits Level 5 is designed for use with the fifth book of any piano method.

Concepts in *Broadway and Movie Hits Level 5*:

Range	Symbols
(musical staff notation)	*ppp*, *pp*, *p*, *mp*, *mf*, *f*, *ff*, ♯, ♭, ♮, *rit.*, *a tempo*, *simile*, *8va*, *loco*, *sempre staccato*, *poco a poco*, *accelerando*, (notation symbols) *cresc.* *decresc.*, *dim.*

Rhythm	Intervals
time signatures: 2/4 4/4 ¢ 6/4 (rhythm notation) swing eighths	2nds, 3rds, 4ths, 5ths, 6ths melodic and harmonic

---

Book: ISBN 1-4234-0062-3
Book/CD: ISBN 1-4234-0391-6

**HAL•LEONARD®
CORPORATION**
7777 W. BLUEMOUND RD. P.O. BOX 13819 MILWAUKEE, WI 53213

Visit Hal Leonard Online at
www.halleonard.com

Full orchestral arrangements, available on CD or GM disk, may be used for both practice and performance:

 TRACKS 9/10 The first track number is a practice tempo. The second track number is the performance tempo.

 TRACK 1 The GM disk has only one track per title and is a preset performance tempo. GM disk tracks can be slowed down to any practice tempo desired, and can also be made faster than the set tempo at will.

Broadway and Movie Hits
Level 5

Table of Contents

Accidentally In Love

from the Motion Picture SHREK 2

Words and Music by
Adam F. Duritz
Arranged by Carol Klose

We're ac - ci - den - tal - ly in love,

ac - ci - den - tal - ly in love, ac - ci - den - tal - ly in

ac - ci - den - tal - ly... Come on, come on, spin a lit - tle tight - er.

Come on, come on, and the world's a lit - tle bright - er. Come on, come on, just get

your - self in - side her love. I'm in love.

decresc. *rit.*

(2'23")

Bless The Beasts And Children

from BLESS THE BEASTS AND CHILDREN

Words and Music by Barry DeVorzon
and Perry Botkin, Jr.
Arranged by Fred Kern

chil - dren, for the world can nev - er be the world they see. Light their way when the dark - ness sur - rounds them. Give them love, let it shine all a - round them.

The Avenue Q Theme

from the Broadway Musical AVENUE Q

Music and Lyrics by Robert Lopez
and Jeff Marx
Arranged by Fred Kern

bills   to   pay. ____   What can you do?   You

work   real   hard and the pay's ____ real low, ____   and   ev - 'ry   ho - ur goes oh ____

____   so   slow, ____   and   at   the   end   of   the day ____ there's no - where to go ____

____   but   home to Av - e - nue Q! ____   You

live on Av - e - nue Q, _____ your friends do, too.

You _____ are twen-ty-two, and you live on Av - e - nue Q.

You live on Av - e - nue Q! You

live on Av - e - nue Q!

(1'03")

13

Cruella De Vil

from Walt Disney's 101 DALMATIANS

Words and Music by
Mel Leven
Arranged by Carol Klose

ice of her stare; _ all in - no - cent chil - dren had bet - ter be - ware. _ She's

like a spi - der wait - ing for the kill. Look out for Cru - el - la De
cresc.

Vil. At first you think Cru - el - la is a dev - il. But
mf

af - ter time has worn a - way the shock, you come to re - a - lize you've

seen her kind of eyes watch-ing you from un-der-neath a rock. This

vam - pire ___ bat, ___ this in - hu - man beast, she ought to be locked _ up and

nev - er re - leased. _ The world was such a whole-some place un - til Cru -

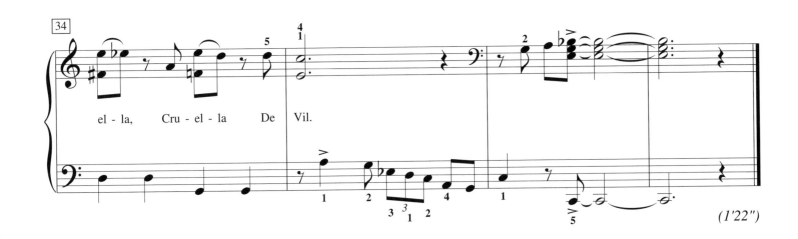

el - la, Cru - el - la De Vil.

(1'22")

Baby Elephant Walk
from the Paramount Picture HATARI!

Words by Hal David
Music by Henry Mancini
Arranged by Mona Rejino

(2'02")

Theme From "Jurassic Park"

from the Universal Motion Picture JURASSIC PARK

Composed by John Williams
Arranged by Mona Rejino

I Have A Dream

from MAMMA MIA!

Words and Music by Benny Andersson
and Bjorn Ulvaeus
Arranged by Carol Klose

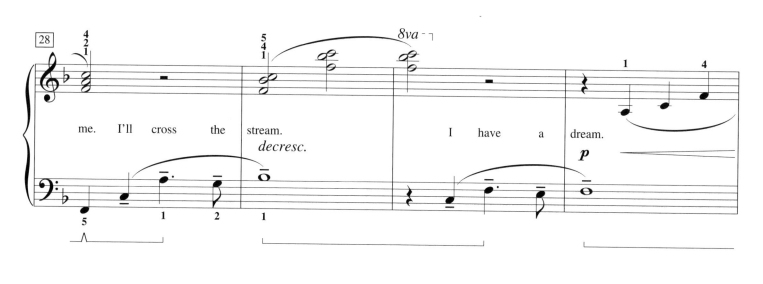

me. I'll cross the stream. *decresc.* I have a dream. *p*

I have a dream, a fan - ta - sy *mf*

to help me through ____ re - al - i - ty. ____

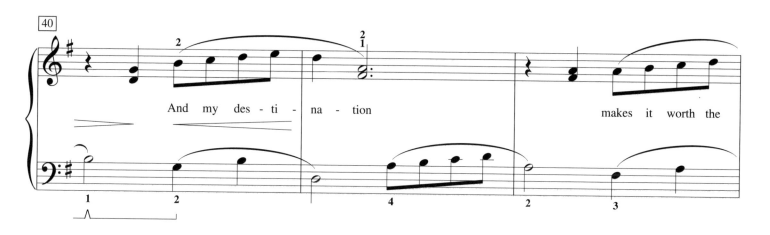

And my des - ti - na - tion makes it worth the

* simply

(2'27")

A Wink And A Smile

featured in the TriStar Motion Picture SLEEPLESS IN SEATTLE

Music by Marc Shaiman
Lyrics by Ramsey McLean
Arranged by Mona Rejino

So you can rev — her up; — and

don't — go slow, — it's on - ly green lights — and "all rights." — Let's go to - geth -

- er _____ with a wink — and a smile. _____

Just the sound of your voice, _ the light in your eyes, _ we're

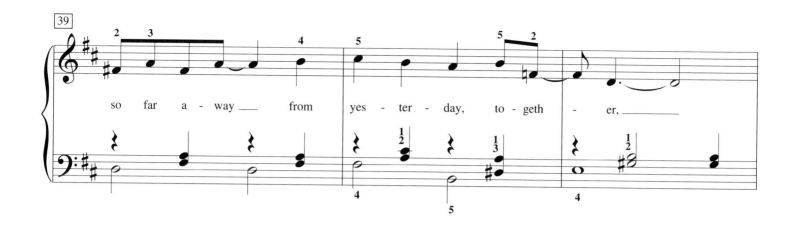

(1'53")

One

from A CHORUS LINE

Music by Marvin Hamlisch
Lyric by Edward Kleban
Arranged by Carol Klose

One smile and sud-den-ly no- bod-y else will do.

You know you'll nev-er be lone - ly with you - know - who.

One mo - ment in her pres - ence and you can for-get the

rest, for the girl is sec- ond best to

none, son. Ooh! Sigh! Give her your at- ten- tion.

33

Do   I   real - ly have   to men - tion,   she's

the   one?

one?

decresc. poco a poco

pp

(2'37")

Wonderful
from WICKED

Music and Lyrics by
Stephen Schwartz
Arranged by Fred Kern

Spirited (♩ = 88)

(1'30")

Till There Was You

from Meredith Willson's THE MUSIC MAN

By Meredith Willson
Arranged by Fred Kern

sky,   but I   nev - er   saw them   wing - ing.   No, I
cresc.

nev - er   saw them   at   all   till   there was   you.
dim.

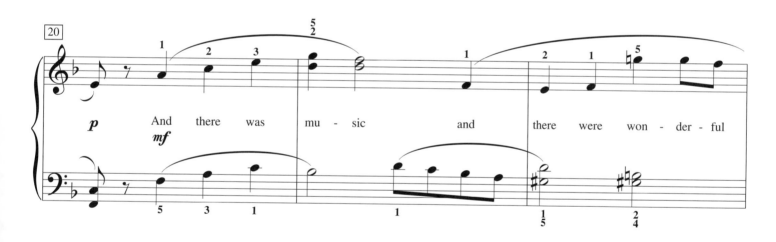

p   And there was   mu - sic   and   there   were   won - der - ful
mf

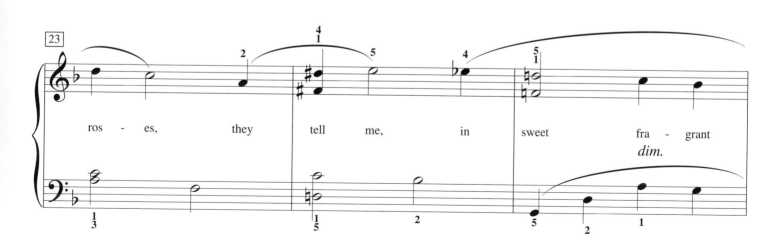

ros - es,   they   tell   me,   in   sweet   fra - grant
dim.

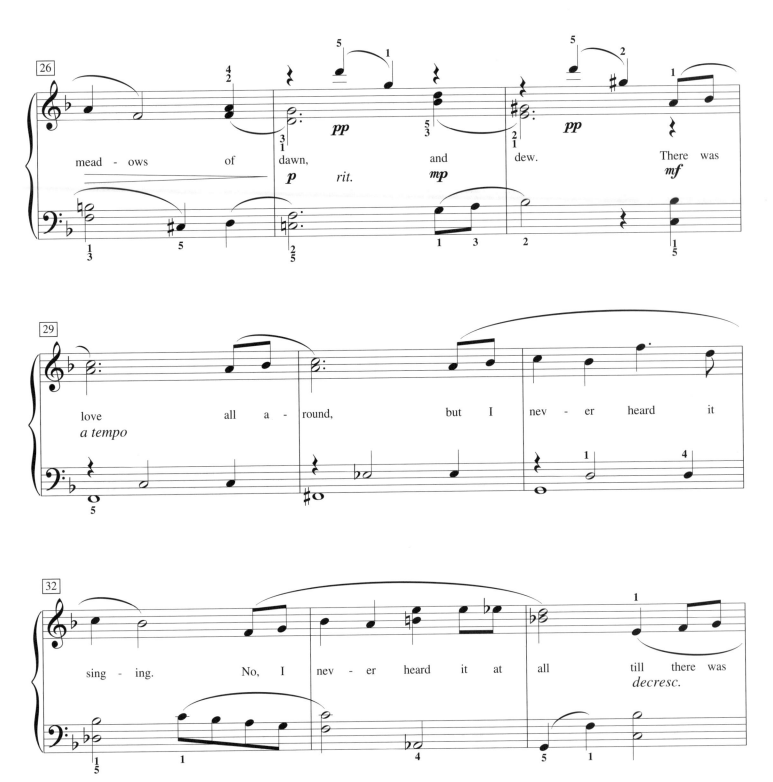

(3'17")